EARTH'S RESOURCES

GEO FACTS

Izzi Howell

Crabtree Publishing Company
www.crabtreebooks.com

Crabtree Publishing Company
www.crabtreebooks.com
1-800-387-7650

Published in Canada
Crabtree Publishing
616 Welland Avenue
St. Catharines, ON
L2M 5V6

Published in the United States
Crabtree Publishing
PMB 59051
350 Fifth Ave, 59th Floor
New York, NY 10118

Published in 2018 by CRABTREE PUBLISHING COMPANY.

First published in 2017 by The Watts Publishing Group
Copyright © The Watts Publishing Group 2017

Author: Izzi Howell

Editors: Izzi Howell, Ellen Rodger

Design: Rocket Design (East Anglia) Ltd

Editorial director: Kathy Middleton

Proofreader: Angela Kaelberer

Prepress technician: Abigail Smith

Print and production coordinator: Margaret Amy Salter

Photographs

Getty: Askold Romanov 9bl, apomares 11, timoph 21t, Nelson Ching/Bloomberg 28b; Shutterstock: Bukhavets Mikhail 4-5, ArtisticPhoto 5t, boyphare 6, Designua 8, 22 and 23t, Christian Vinces 9t, Mikadun 9br, VectorPot 10, Andrew Rybalko 12, KYTan 13, pupunkkop 15, Richard Thornton 17, Nucleartist 18, Syndromeda 19, Pretty Vectors 20t, humphery 20b, travelpeter 22b, Bernhard Staehli 23b, Faber14 24t, SkyPics Studio 24b, Constantine Androsoff 25t, KittyVector 25bl, Bukhavets Mikhail 25br, MikeDotta 26t, Crystal Eye Studio 26b, OVKNHR 27, avian 28t, canadastock 29.

All design elements from Shutterstock, including Alfmaler, sergio34, sub job, DRogatnev, NadiiaZ, kolotuschenko, petovarga, A7880S, Doloves, Meilun and Alex Oakenman.

Every attempt has been made to clear copyright. Should there be any inadvertent omission, please apply to the publisher for rectification.

Printed in the USA/122019/BG20171102

Library and Archives Canada Cataloguing in Publication

Howell, Izzi, author
        Earth's resources geo facts / Izzi Howell.

(Geo facts)
Includes index.
Issued in print and electronic formats.
ISBN 978-0-7787-4383-5 (hardcover).--
ISBN 978-0-7787-4398-9 (softcover).--
ISBN 978-1-4271-2016-8 (HTML)

        1. Natural resources--Juvenile literature. 2. Conservation of natural resources--Juvenile literature. I. Title.

HC85.H69 2018   j333.7   C2017-906903-9
                                                       C2017-906904-7

Library of Congress Cataloging-in Publication Data

Names: Howell, Izzi, author.
Title: Earth's resources geo facts / Izzi Howell.
Description: New York, New York : Crabtree Publishing, 2018. |
Series: Geo facts | Includes index. |
Identifiers: LCCN 2017050653 (print) | LCCN 2017054198 (ebook) |
    ISBN 9781427120168 (Electronic HTML) |
    ISBN 9780778743835 (reinforced library binding) |
    ISBN 9780778743989 (pbk.)
Subjects: LCSH: Natural resources--Juvenile literature. | Conservation of natural resources--Juvenile literature.
Classification: LCC HC85 (ebook) | LCC HC85 .H68 2018 (print) | DDC 333.7--dc23
LC record available at https://lccn.loc.gov/2017050653

Contents

What are Resources? 4

Resources Around the World 6

Mining 8

FOCUS ON Aluminum 10

Wood 12

FOCUS ON Rainforest Deforestation 14

Water 16

Food and Farms 18

FOCUS ON GM Crops 20

FOCUS ON North Sea Fishing 21

Fossil Fuels 22

Renewable Energy 24

Garbage and Recycling 26

FOCUS ON Eco-cities 28

Glossary 30

Test Yourself 31

Index 32

What are Resources?

There are many natural resources on Earth that we can use to make objects, support ourselves, or produce energy. Wood, metal, and stone are used for construction. Fossil fuels, running water, and sunlight can be used to produce electricity.

Renewable resources

Wind, sunlight, and water are described as **renewable** resources. Our supply of these resources will naturally renew, no matter how much we use of them. Wood and other resources that can be regrown quickly and easily are also renewable. However, humans have to make sure they replant and replace these resources, so that they have a supply in the future.

Radioactive material (page 27)

Rubber (page 12)

Coal (page 8)

Metal (page 8)

Stone (page 8)

Precious stones (page 8)

North Americans use

198 pounds (90 kg)

of natural resources from Earth every day.

Non-renewable resources

Many resources on Earth, such as coal, oil, and minerals, are **non-renewable**. Once we use up our supply of these resources, it will take millions of years for the resources to naturally form again.

Oil wells pump oil from reserves deep underground.

At the moment, we have enough oil to last us for around 50 more years.

Animals
(page 18)

Wood
(page 12)

Plants
(page 18)

Gas
(page 22)

Oil
(page 22)

Water
(page 16)

Using resources

It's important that humans use resources in a responsible and **sustainable** way. We need to share resources fairly so that everyone on Earth has access to the resources that they need. Restricting our use of some resources now will allow us to leave enough for future generations. We also need to be careful that we do not gather or process resources in a way that harms the natural environment.

Resources Around the World

Some countries consume far more resources than others. The amount of resources used by a country depends on its income.

Different incomes

Wealthier countries use the most resources. People in these countries own more things such as electronics and cars. They live in bigger homes that use more energy. They eat more food and use more water than people in poorer countries.

x1

x10

People in wealthier countries use

10 times

more resources than people in poorer countries.

Gathering resources

Many resources are **extracted** in poorer countries. People extract **raw** materials, such as minerals and **timber**. They also grow crops. These jobs are known as primary sector jobs. People who work in primary sector jobs often earn low wages and work many hours in difficult conditions.

This man in Thailand is cutting a large tree into smaller planks of wood.

Processing resources

Once a resource has been gathered, it needs to be processed into a product that we can use. For example, planks of wood are cut from logs, and plastic is made from oil. People who process resources work in the secondary sector. Building objects from materials, such as making a car from metal and plastic, is also a secondary sector job.

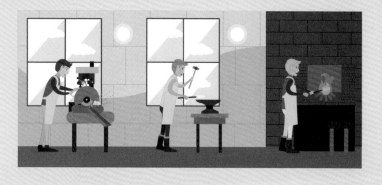

Managing resources

Tertiary sector jobs deal with the management of resources. Some people who work in the tertiary sector own the factories that process resources, organize the shipping of resources, or sell them to other people. These jobs are relatively well paid. They are often done by people who live in wealthier countries.

Main export of countries

This map shows the main resource/material export of countries around the world.

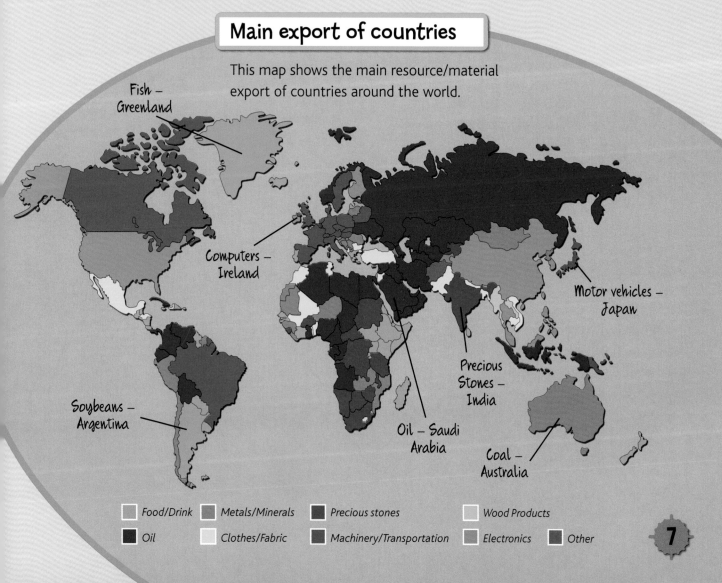

Fish – Greenland

Computers – Ireland

Motor vehicles – Japan

Precious Stones – India

Soybeans – Argentina

Oil – Saudi Arabia

Coal – Australia

Food/Drink Metals/Minerals Precious stones Wood Products

Oil Clothes/Fabric Machinery/Transportation Electronics Other

Mining

Mining is the removal of rocks and minerals from the surface of Earth. Stone for construction, precious gems such as diamonds, and different metals are all collected through mining.

Uses

Mined resources are used in many ways. As well as construction, different metals are used in cell phones, TVs, lightbulbs, and computers. Drills for cutting bricks and concrete sometimes have diamond tips. Gold pieces are often used in electrical circuits.

Surface mining

One of the simplest types of mining is surface mining. Miners remove layers of soil and rock to access deeper layers that contain valuable resources such as coal. The hole created is called a **quarry**. Surface mining is easiest for miners, as they do not have to work deep underground. Rocks such as limestone and marble are usually cut from quarries.

soil/rock

coal

soil/rock

Quarries can be seen cut into the hillside.

Underground mining

Some resources can only be gathered from underground mines. Miners use machines to dig tunnels to access resources buried deep below the surface. In the past, miners had to dig all underground tunnels and cut away rock by hand. They worked in dangerous, hot conditions. Today, conditions in underground mines are better, but in some countries, miners still work in unsafe tunnels.

These miners in Bolivia are placing explosives that will blow up a section of the rock wall. Then they will transport the smaller pieces of rock for processing.

Processing

Many resources that come from mines have to be processed before they can be used. Some metals combine with other minerals to make **ores**. To remove a metal from an ore, the ore is heated until the metal separates from the other minerals.

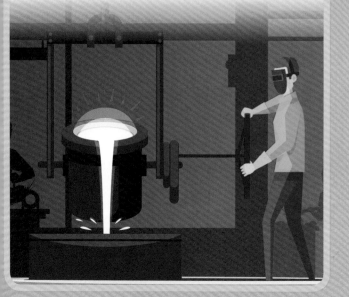

Environmental impact

Mining can have a negative impact on the environment. Surface mines destroy the habitats of many animals and plants. If underground mines are not supported properly, they can collapse inward. This creates a sinkhole. The chemicals used in mining and waste from ore processing are often dumped nearby and not cleaned up properly. They poison the land and the water supply, causing great harm to plants, animals, and humans.

The water in this lake has been polluted by copper mining.

FOCUS ON Aluminum

Aluminum is a soft, lightweight metal that is often used in vehicles and buildings. It is a common metal, making up around eight percent of Earth's crust.

Uses

Aluminum is a very useful metal. It is strong, flexible, and does not rust. It is commonly used to make aircraft and trains, as well as window frames. Most people have aluminum food and drink cans and aluminum foil in their homes.

Ore

Aluminum is rarely found in its pure form. It is a very reactive metal, and it nearly always reacts with other minerals to form an ore called bauxite. Bauxite forms close to the surface, so miners extract it from quarries, rather than tunneling underground.

Location

Bauxite ore is found all over the world. The largest bauxite mines are in Australia, Brazil, China, and Guinea. In these countries, bauxite quarries have destroyed large areas of rain forest and other natural habitats.

In this bauxite mine in Venezuela, large areas of the tree-covered mountains have been stripped away so that miners can get the bauxite underneath.

Processing bauxite

Extracting aluminum from bauxite is a complicated process that uses a lot of electricity. Some companies build processing plants in areas with cheaper electricity, such as Iceland. Iceland gets its electricity from **geothermal energy** (see page 25). However, many processing plants run on fossil fuels, which damage the environment.

Recycling aluminum only requires

5 percent

of the energy that it takes to make new aluminum from bauxite ore. For this reason, it is much better for the environment for us to recycled aluminum.

Recycling

Recycling aluminum uses far less electricity than creating new aluminum. To recycle aluminum, old aluminum products are melted down and formed into sheets. These sheets are then used to make new products. Recycling aluminum also means that less bauxite needs to be mined, which causes less damage to the environment.

Wood

Wood is a common resource that can be used in many different ways. Our supply of wood must be carefully managed, as removing too many trees can harm the natural environment.

Uses

We can use pieces of wood to build houses and furniture. We can also burn wood as a fuel. There are resources in other parts of a tree, such as its fruit and its **sap**. Sap from the maple tree can be made into maple syrup and sap from the rubber tree can be processed into rubber.

Processing

Wood used for building is called timber. Some logs are cut by hand using chain saws. Other wood is cut to size by huge industrial saws in a timber mill. The sawdust and scraps of wood that are left behind are glued together to make chipboard. Chipboard is much cheaper than wood, but it isn't as strong.

Deforestation

People cut down around 15 billion trees every year. Some of this wood is used as a resource, while some woodland areas are cleared so that the land can be used in other ways. Many woodland areas are cleared to make room for agriculture. When a forest is cut down and not replanted with trees, it is known as **deforestation**.

Replanting

Some cleared forest areas are replanted with more trees. In doing so, we can guarantee our supply of wood for the future. However, many areas are not replanted with the same trees that were cut down. People plant fast-growing trees, such as pines, that will quickly grow big enough to be cut down again. Rubber and palm trees, from which rubber and palm oil can be gathered, are also popular trees to plant.

Biodiversity

When people cut down forests and plant different species of trees in their place, it destroys the forest **ecosystem**. The new trees may not provide the right habitat or type of food for forest animals. Most old forests are very **biodiverse**, with many species of plants and animals. This biodiversity is lost when only one species of tree is replanted.

This area has been cleared of woodland to plant new palm trees for palm oil.

Carbon dioxide

Replanting trees helps the environment. Trees, and all plants, absorb **carbon dioxide** (CO_2). If we cut down trees without replanting them, there will be fewer trees to absorb carbon dioxide. The level of carbon dioxide in the atmosphere then goes up. This has a negative impact on the climate of Earth (see page 23).

One tree absorbs around 48 pounds (22 kg) of CO_2 every year.

That's the same amount as one car releases by driving 11 miles (18 km).

It would take 706 trees to absorb the average amount of CO_2 released by one car every year.

Rainforest Deforestation

Deforestation happens all over the world, but tropical rain forests are some of the most affected areas. If the current rate of deforestation continues, we will destroy all the rain forests within the next 100 years.

Tropical hardwood

Loggers cut down rainforest trees such as mahogany, ebony, and teak. The wood from these trees is valued for its beauty and strength and can be sold for a much higher price than other types of wood. Many loggers work illegally, gathering more wood than they are allowed. They destroy large areas of rain forest to build roads to reach the trees.

35 cubic feet (1 m³) of mahogany is worth over **$1,582.**

Rainforest resources

Rain forests are home to many valuable resources besides wood, including fruits, nuts, and spices. Many rainforest plants are used in life-saving medicines, such as those that treat cancer. Some farmers plant coffee, banana, and avocado trees among wild rainforest trees without damaging the natural habitat. If a product has a Rainforest Alliance label, it means that it has been grown in a sustainable way.

Slash and burn

Many farmers clear rain forests using a technique called slash and burn. They chop down the rainforest trees and plants and then burn them. The ash from the burned plants **fertilizes** the soil so it is suitable for crops. However, the soil only stays fertile for a few years. If farmers cannot afford fertilizer for their fields, they abandon their land and clear more space through slash and burn.

Burning plants and trees releases carbon dioxide. This leads to global warming (see page 23).

This land in Thailand has been cleared through slashing and burning.

Cattle farming

Large areas of rain forest in South America are cleared to make room for cattle farms. Meat from the cattle raised on these farms is sent to shops across South America. Some of it is shipped to other continents around the world. However, cleared rainforest land is not a particularly good place for cattle to live. Grass does not grow well in the poor rainforest soil, so food has to be brought in for the cattle to eat.

Over 60%
of rainforest land that is cleared in Brazil is used for cattle farming.

The future

The governments of some countries are working hard to preserve the rain forests and stop their resources from being destroyed. The Brazilian government has promised to replant over 46,332 square miles (120,000 sq. km) of rain forest by 2030. Other governments are working to stop illegal logging and to protect the habitats of rainforest plants and animals.

Water

Water is one of the most important resources on Earth. We use water in many ways in our homes, on farms, and in different industries. However, there are many people around the world who do not have access to a clean and reliable water supply.

Water on Earth

Over 70 percent of Earth's surface is covered in water. However, most of this water is salt water. Only 3 percent of the water on Earth is fresh water, which we can use for drinking, household use, and agriculture.

Uses

Wealthy countries use much more water than poor countries. People in wealthier countries use more water in their homes than people in other countries. They have access to baths and showers, washing machines, and dishwashers. All of these use water. In poorer countries, most water is used in agriculture to **irrigate** crops in the fields.

Amount of water used per person per day:

USA: 155 gallons (590 L) a day

India: 38 gallons (144 L) a day

Mali: 2.9 gallons (11 L) a day

Gathering water

People gather water from above and below the ground. Fresh water can be taken from lakes, rivers, and **reservoirs** (artificial lakes). Water also soaks through the ground and fills the space between soil and rocks. This water can be accessed through springs or by digging a well.

Safe water

Water often needs to be processed so that it is safe for humans to drink or use. It is filtered and mixed with chemicals that kill dangerous bacteria. This process is also used to clean dirty water that leaves our homes through sewage pipes. Once this dirty water has been cleaned, it can be released back into rivers and lakes.

Drought

We will never run out of water, as it is a renewable resource. However, **global warming** (see page 23) and our growing population put pressure on our supply of water. Changes to our climate mean that many places are experiencing **drought**. Less rain means that it is harder for farmers to irrigate their crops. It can also be hard for farmers to find enough water to irrigate the huge fields of crops needed to support a large population.

Some crops, such as almond trees, require much more water than other crops. It takes 1.3 gallons (5 L) of water to grow one almond.

Access to water

In high-income countries, most homes are connected to a safe drinking water supply. However, many people in low- and middle-income countries have to travel a long way to access water. In some cases, their only water supply may be untreated, dirty water from a river or lake. Drinking dirty water leads to many dangerous, and even fatal, diseases.

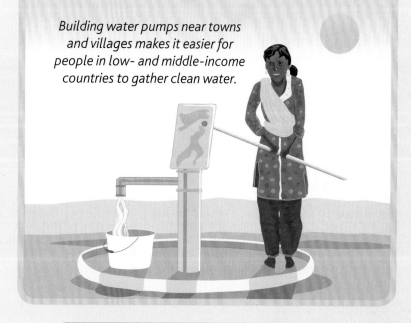

Building water pumps near towns and villages makes it easier for people in low- and middle-income countries to gather clean water.

Reducing water use

Using less water saves money and is good for the environment. Some ways of using less water in the home are collecting rainwater to water plants, fixing leaks, and installing toilets that run on recycled bathwater. In industry, factories can reuse water. We can also stop wasting water on non-essential uses, such as watering the grass on golf courses to keep them green.

Food and Farms

There are not enough wild plants and animals on Earth to provide food for our population. Instead, we grow crops and raise animals on farms.

History

The first humans were hunter-gatherers, who moved from place to place looking for wild food to eat. They could not find enough food to support a large number of people, so the human population was small. When humans began to settle in one place and grow food on farms, they could produce large amounts of food. This allowed the human population on Earth to grow much bigger.

Grains

Wheat, rice, corn, and other grains are some of the most commonly grown crops around the world. These foods make up the main part of many people's diets. They provide carbohydrates that give people energy. Farmers often use tractors to clear their fields, plant seeds, and harvest their crops.

Livestock

Farmers raise animals such as cattle, sheep, pigs, and chickens for their meat, milk, and eggs. Many farmers keep their **livestock** in closed barns so that it is easier to feed them. Once the animal is large enough to be killed, it is taken to a slaughterhouse. The meat is then processed and shipped to be sold.

Import and export

Crops are not always used to feed the people in the area where they are grown. Many crops are grown in poorer countries and then sold to wealthier countries. Farmers make more money by exporting one type of crop than by growing different foods for people in their country. However, sending crops around the world by plane and truck releases **greenhouse gases** (see page 23) and pollution.

Many farmers in Tanzania, Africa, grow coffee as a cash crop. A cash crop is a crop grown to make money, rather than to provide food for a community.

Food quality

Some people worry about the quality of food that they buy. Many farmers spray their crops with **pesticides** so that insects don't eat the plants. Some people believe that these pesticides are dangerous for humans, so they buy organic food that is grown without pesticides. Other people think that it's cruel for farmers to keep livestock in small, enclosed barns, so they buy free range meat and dairy products. Free range animals are allowed to spend some time outside.

Sharing food

Today, there are still many people around the world who do not have access to enough food. However, this is not because we cannot grow enough food for everyone. Instead, it is because we do not share food equally around the world. In some places, a huge amount of uneaten food is thrown away. Other people are not paid enough money to buy food to support themselves.

FOCUS ON GM Crops

Genetically modifying, or changing, crops is one way of increasing the amount of food we have available. However, some people believe that the risks of GM crops are greater than the benefits.

Changes

Genetically modified (GM) crops are crops that have been changed so that they are easier to grow and less likely to die. Some GM crops are changed to make them less likely to be affected by pests, plant diseases, or droughts. Other GM crops grow bigger than normal crops or produce more fruit. This means that they can feed more people.

Global hunger

Around one in nine people around the world suffer from hunger. In some cases this is because they can't grow enough crops to support themselves or their crops die from a disease. GM crops are one way of helping these people grow enough food to avoid hunger.

Concerns

Some people are worried about GM crops. They aren't sure if planting GM crops is good for the environment or if eating GM crops is safe. They believe that there are other ways to solve world hunger. These include sharing resources more fairly and encouraging countries to grow crops for themselves rather than selling them to other countries.

This rice crop has failed because of drought.

North Sea Fishing

Fish are one of the few wild foods that most people eat. Up until the 1900s, many species of fish lived in the North Sea. There were large numbers of mackerel, salmon, cod, and herring. However, overfishing has shrunk the fish population in this area.

North Sea

Overfishing

Many fishermen in the North Sea use huge trawler nets, which they drag across the water, catching anything in their path. These nets allow them to catch a large number of fish. In the past, fishermen sometimes caught far more fish than they needed. They didn't leave enough fish to breed and replace those that had been lost. For years, there were far fewer fish to catch.

This boat is using a trawler net to fish for crabs in the North Sea.

Consequences

Trawler nets accidentally kill many large ocean animals, such as dolphins and porpoises. They also damage the seabed and kill many ocean plants. When a species of fish has been overfished, it affects the food chain. Predators that usually eat the fish go hungry and can die as well.

Solutions

Some fishermen use special trawler nets that large sea mammals or small young fish can escape from. If fishermen leave the young fish to grow up, their supply of fish is guaranteed for the future. Fish can also be raised on fish farms, while wild fish populations are left to recover.

Fossil Fuels

Fossil fuels, such as coal, oil, and gas, are natural resources that we use for energy. There is a limited amount of fossil fuels left on Earth. They may run out during our lifetime.

Formation and location

Fossil fuels were formed over millions of years from the remains of dead plants and animals. Today, they can be found underground. Companies drill deep underground to find pockets of liquid oil and gases, such as methane. They build huge oil wells to pump out the oil and gas. Many oil wells are located on the sea bed. Coal is dug out from between layers of rock in mines.

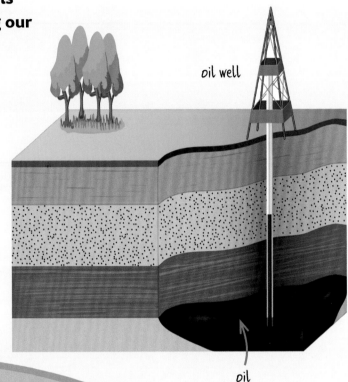

oil well

oil

Uses

Fossil fuels are commonly burned in power plants to generate electricity. The burning fuel produces heat, which is used to boil water. The boiling water makes steam, which is used to turn a turbine. The moving turbine powers a generator, which produces electricity. Oil can also be made into gasoline for cars and other vehicles or processed into plastic.

41 percent of electricity is currently produced by coal-fired power plants.

electricity production

plastics

fuel for vehicles

Greenhouse gases

Burning oil and coal produces carbon dioxide, which is a greenhouse gas. Other greenhouse gases include methane and water vapor, or steam. Methane is produced by animals. It is also found underwater. Greenhouse gases gather in the atmosphere. They trap heat from Earth and stop it from escaping into space. This makes the temperature on Earth increase.

greenhouses gases   heat from the Sun

Global warming

The increase in the temperature on Earth is known as global warming. Global warming is affecting Earth's climate and weather. Some areas are experiencing drier weather. This makes it harder for people to grow enough food, as most crops need regular water to thrive. The ice at the poles is melting in the warm weather. The melted water released into the ocean is making the sea level rise. Many places are at risk of flooding.

16 of the 17 warmest years on record have happened since 2001.

The edge of this melting glacier in Antarctica is falling into the sea.

! Earth's climate does naturally go through warmer and cooler periods. However, 97 percent of scientists agree that the current climate change is due to human activity.

Acid rain

Burning fossil fuels releases acidic chemicals that mix with water in the atmosphere. This falls to the ground as acid rain. Acid rain poisons lakes, rivers, and forests and can kill the animals that live in these habitats.

Renewable Energy

Renewable sources of energy, such as the wind, water, and sunlight, will probably never run out. They can be used to generate large amounts of electricity over a long period of time. Some renewable energy sources are also clean energy sources, which do not release any carbon dioxide or pollution into the atmosphere.

Sunlight

Solar energy is produced by solar panels, which convert light from the Sun into electricity. People can use several small solar panels to produce electricity for their homes. Huge fields of giant panels set up in sunny places can generate electricity to power factories and cities. However, there are several drawbacks, including the high cost and need for sunny, bright weather.

! The amount of sunlight that hits Earth in one hour could provide enough energy for the world to live on for one year.

Wind

When the wind moves the sails on a wind turbine, the spinning movement powers a generator that generates electricity. Some people use individual wind turbines to power their homes or businesses. Most wind turbines are placed in large groups called wind farms. Wind farms are usually built at sea or in isolated places, where there is a lot of wind.

Water

The movement of water can be used to generate electricity. As water moves through a dam or because of waves or tides, it can spin a turbine. As in wind power, this turbine powers a generator, which generates electricity. However, water turbines can destroy the habitats of water animals and plants.

The falling water in this dam powers a hydroelectric power plant.

Biomass

This energy source is made from rotting plants or animal waste. Biomass can be burned to produce heat or to power machines that generate electricity. It can even be mixed with chemicals to produce fuel for vehicles. Biomass is a renewable energy source because plants can be regrown quickly and easily. However, the burning of biomass releases carbon dioxide and other polluting gases. This makes it a less environmentally friendly option.

Geothermal energy

In volcanic areas, the natural heat of Earth can be used to generate electricity. This is known as geothermal energy. To generate energy, water is sent underground. There, it is naturally heated by magma and becomes steam. This steam can be used to heat buildings or power a turbine to make electricity.

Garbage and Recycling

Every day, we create a huge amount of waste in our homes and in factories. Finding ways to reduce and recycle trash helps us to use fewer resources and keep our planet clean.

Landfill

Most of the garbage that we produce is buried in large holes in the ground, called **landfill** sites. The trash in landfill sites is usually a mixture of food waste, plastic, tins, glass, and broken objects. Most of this waste will stay in the ground for thousands of years before it breaks down. Some waste also releases dangerous chemicals that poison the soil.

This worker is dumping garbage on a landfill site in Italy.

Plastics

Plastic is a versatile material that we use in many ways, from bags and boxes to pens and furniture. Most of the plastic products that we use end up in landfills or in the ocean. Plastic in the ocean pollutes ocean habitats and kills ocean animals.

Every year, we throw away enough plastic to circle Earth **four times.**

Biodegradable waste

Food, plant, and animal waste is **biodegradable**. This means that it will quickly break down into soil. Some people collect their food waste to make into compost for their gardens. In other places, the city or town collects people's food waste and trash at the same time. Separating biodegradable waste from the main garbage helps to reduce the amount of waste that goes to landfills.

ORGANIC   PLASTIC   BATTERIES   GLASS   METAL   PAPER

Recycling

Many materials can be recycled, including glass, paper, plastic, cardboard, and metal. Some people sort their recyclable waste themselves by putting it into different recycling bins. In other places, waste is sorted by hand in large factories. Recycling plants can use magnets to separate different metals.

Some parts of electronic devices can be recycled. This man is separating recyclable parts at an electronic recycling plant in Turkey.

Energy and recycling

Recycling materials does require some electricity and can release greenhouse gases. However, recycling materials always uses less energy than making new materials from scratch.

Recycling plastic uses 70 percent less energy than making new plastic.

Reducing waste

It's much easier to reduce the amount of waste that you create than to recycle waste. You can carry a reusable bag to use when shopping, rather than using disposable plastic bags. Buying fruit and vegetables without plastic packaging is another way to reduce waste.

Nuclear waste

Nuclear power plants use **radioactive** materials to generate energy. This process produces dangerous, radioactive waste. If this waste is placed in the ground, it poisons the soil and water and can kill living things. Nuclear waste must be buried deep underground or in a concrete case to stop it from damaging the environment.

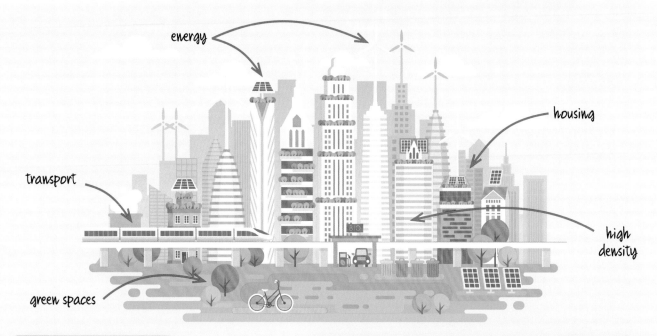

FOCUS ON Eco-cities

Eco-cities are cleverly planned and built to use fewer resources in a sustainable way. A large number of people can live in an eco-city without having a negative impact on the environment.

- energy
- housing
- transport
- high density
- green spaces

Old and new

Many eco-cities are old cities that are gradually adapting to become more environmentally friendly. The city of Freiburg in Germany has become an eco-city by building solar power plants, improving its public transport system, and helping people to recycle. In some countries, new eco-cities are being built from scratch. Many newly-built Chinese eco-cities have excellent public transportation links, eco-friendly housing, and green industries from the start.

This is a model of the Tianjin eco-city, which is currently under construction in China. It will eventually be home to 250,000 people and should be finished by the year 2020.

Housing

Building eco-friendly houses helps residents to use less energy. If houses are well insulated, people won't need to use as much gas and electricity for heating and cooling. Some houses have water systems that recycle used water to flush toilets. Others have solar panels to generate their own electricity.

Transport

Cars are not an environmentally friendly transportation option. Currently, most run on fossil fuels and produce air pollution. Eco-cities spend more on public transportation such as trains and subways than on building roads just for cars. Some trains and subways run on electricity, which means that they do not pollute as much. Walking and biking are the greenest forms of transportation. Many eco-cities build bike paths to encourage their residents to use their bikes.

There are tram services and over 310 miles (500 km) of bike paths in the eco-city of Freiburg, Germany.

Waste

Eco-cities can set up recycling programs to help their residents reduce waste. In some cities, recyclables, such as paper and cans, are collected from homes and businesses. Food waste is also collected and made into compost to fertilize farm fields.

High density

Eco-cities are often high **density** areas, meaning they have a lot of people living in a small area. This helps the city to be more environmentally friendly and use fewer resources. It takes less energy and building supplies to build and maintain one block of apartments than multiple large houses. If cities are small, it's also easier for residents to commute to their jobs by public transport or on foot.

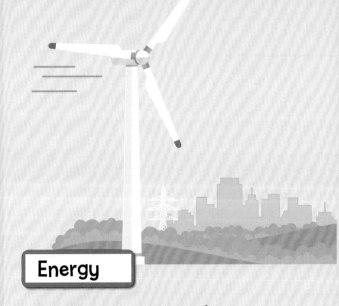

Energy

Eco-cities try to get as much electricity as possible from sustainable and environmentally friendly energy sources, such as solar, wind, or tidal power. This reduces pollution and the amount of greenhouse gases released into the atmosphere. The construction of new solar, wind, or tidal power plants provides jobs for local residents. This is good for the **economy**.

Green spaces

Although eco-cities can be densely populated, it's also important for city planners to include parks and other green areas where wildlife can live. Plants absorb carbon dioxide, which helps to keep the air clean. Urban farms, built inside the city, provide food for residents. Food from local farms is cheaper and better for the environment, as it does not need to be transported by trucks.

Glossary

biodegradable Describes something that will quickly break down naturally

biodiverse Having a large number of species of plants and animals in an area

carbon dioxide A gas that is made by burning carbon or breathed out by humans and animals

crust The outer layer of Earth

deforestation When forests are cut down and not replanted

density The number of people living in an area

drought A long period when there is not enough rain and people do not have enough water

economy The money made and used by a country

ecosystem The way in which living things interact in their environment

extracted Removed

fertilize To add something to the soil to make crops grow better

fossil fuel A fuel, such as coal, gas or oil, which is from under the ground

geothermal energy A type of energy powered by the heat from Earth

global warming An increase in the temperature on Earth

greenhouse gas A gas that traps heat in Earth's atmosphere

irrigate To water crops

landfill A place where garbage is buried in the ground

livestock Animals kept on a farm for their meat or other produce

logger A person who cuts down trees for wood

non-renewable Describes a resource that cannot be replaced once it has been used

ore A rock from which metal can be extracted

pesticide A chemical that kills mainly insects that eat plants on farms

quarry A place where stone or other materials are cut from a large hole in the ground

radioactive Something that has or produces energy from the breaking up of atoms

raw Not processed

renewable Describes a resource that can be replaced once it has been used

reservoir An artificial lake

sap The liquid inside plants and trees

sustainable Describes something that does not damage the environment and so can continue for a long time

timber Wood that has been processed and cut

Test yourself!

1. Name two non-renewable resources.

2. What is the name of aluminum ore?

3. What is slash and burn?

4. What is a cash crop?

5. What percentage of electricity in the world is currently produced by coal-fired power plants?

6. Name a greenhouse gas.

7. Where does the energy in geothermal energy come from?

8. Why is plastic in the ocean dangerous?

! Check your answers on page 32.

Further reading

***Source to Resource* series**
Michael Bright (Crabtree, 2016)

***Energy Revolution* series**
(Crabtree, 2010)

Living in a Sustainable Way (Next Generation Energy)
Megan Kopp (Crabtree, 2016)

Websites

Read more about resources at the following websites:

www.dkfindout.com/uk/earth/rocks-and-minerals/metals-from-rocks/

climatekids.nasa.gov/menu/energy/

www.sciencekids.co.nz/sciencefacts/recycling.html

Index

acid rain 23
aluminum 10–11

biomass 25

carbon dioxide 13, 15, 23, 24,
    25, 29
climate change 13, 17, 23
coal 5, 7, 8, 22, 23
crops 6, 15, 16, 17, 18, 19, 20,
    23

deforestation 12, 14–15
drought 17, 20

eco-cities 28–29

farms 14, 15, 16, 17, 18, 19,
    29
fishing 7, 21
fossil fuels 4, 11, 22–23, 29

geothermal energy 11, 25
global warming 15, 17, 23
GM crops 20
greenhouse gases 19, 23, 27,
    29

habitats 9, 11, 13, 14, 15, 23,
    25, 26

landfill 26
livestock 18, 19

metal 4, 7, 8, 9, 10, 11, 27
minerals 5, 6, 8, 9, 10
mining 8–9, 10, 11, 22

non-renewable resources 5
nuclear waste 27

oil 5, 7, 22, 23
ore 9, 10, 11

palm oil 13
plastic 7, 22, 26, 27
poorer countries 6, 16, 17, 19
quarries 8, 10, 11

rain forests 11, 14, 15
recycling 11, 17, 26–27, 28, 29
renewable resources 4, 17, 24,
    25
rubber 12, 13

slash and burn 15
stone 4, 8, 9
sunlight 4, 23, 24

water 4, 6, 9, 16–17, 21, 22,
    23, 25, 27, 28
wealthier countries 6, 7, 16,
    17, 19
wind 4, 24, 25, 29
wood 4, 6, 7, 12–13, 14, 15

Answers

1 Coal, oil, or minerals

2 Bauxite

3 Chopping down and then
   burning trees to clear space
   for farming

4 A crop grown to make money,
   rather than to provide food for
   a community

5 41 percent

6 Carbon dioxide, methane, or
   water vapor

7 The natural heat of Earth

8 It pollutes ocean habitats and
   kills ocean animals